Cosmos Chronicles

Trailblazing Space Scientists

Rachael L. Thomas

Lerner Publications ◆ Minneapolis

Lerner Publications Company
A division of Lerner Publishing Group, Inc.
241 First Avenue North
Minneapolis, MN 55401 USA

For reading levels and more information, look up this title at www.lernerbooks.com.

Main body text set in Caecilia LT Std 11.25/20
Typeface provided by Adobe Systems.

Photo Acknowledgements
The images in this book are used with permission of: © NASA, pp. 4–5, 6, 7 (bottom), 9, 10, 11, 12, 14, 15 (top), 15 (bottom), 29 (bottom); © Thomas Pesquet/ESA/NASA/Flickr, p. 5; © Robert Markowitz/NASA, p. 7 (top); © Alfred Pasieka/Science Photo Library/Getty Images, p. 8; © Everystockphoto.com/NASA, p. 13 (bottom); © NASA Johnson/Flickr, p. 13 (top); © Official SpaceX Photos/Flickr, p. 16 (left, right); © OnInnovation/Flickr, p. 17 (bottom); © SpaceX/Wikimedia Commons, p. 17 (top); © Rattiya Thongdumhyu/Shutterstock Images, p. 18; © Archive.org/NASA/Marshall Space Flight Center, p. 19 (top); © Bettmann/Getty Images, p. 19 (middle); © Getty Images, p. 19 (bottom); © NASA/Wikimedia Commons, p. 20 (left); © BioServe Space Technologies/NASA, p. 21 (top); © Leigh Vogel/Getty Images, p. 21 (bottom); © NASA/JPL-Caltech, pp. 22, 23 (top, bottom); © X-ray: NASA/UMass/D. Wang et al., IR: NASA/STScI, p. 24; © ESA/C. Carreau/NASA, p. 25 (top); © Frederick M. Brown/Getty Images, p. 25 (bottom); © NASA's Goddard Space Flight Center, pp. 26–27; © NASA HQ PHOTO/Flickr, p. 27; © NASA Earth Observatory, p. 28; © Bruce Fingerhood/Flickr, p. 29 (top).

Cover: © NASA
Design elements: © NASA/JPL-Caltech/STScI/IRAM

Library of Congress Cataloging-in-Publication Data

Names: Thomas, Rachael L., author.
Title: Trailblazing space scientists / by Rachael L. Thomas.
Description: Minneapolis : Lerner Publications, [2019] | Series: Cosmos chronicles | Audience: Ages 8–12. | Audience: Grades 4 to 6. | Includes bibliographical references and index.
Identifiers: LCCN 2018058312 (print) | LCCN 2019002405 (ebook) | ISBN 9781541556430 (eb pdf) | ISBN 9781541555952 (lb : alk. paper) | ISBN 9781541573727 (pb : alk. paper)
Subjects: LCSH: International Space Station—Juvenile literature. | Space sciences—Research—Juvenile literature. | Space environment—Experiments—Juvenile literature. | Astronauts—Juvenile literature. | Outer space—Exploration—Juvenile literature.
Classification: LCC TL797.15 (ebook) | LCC TL797.15 .T46 2019 (print) | DDC 629.45—dc23

LC record available at https://lccn.loc.gov/2018058312

Manufactured in the United States of America
1 – CG – 7/15/19

Contents

Science Among the Stars

What do you want to know about space? Scientists are likely trying to find an answer! Each year scientists perform hundreds of experiments in space.

These experiments take days, weeks, or even years to plan. Space has **extreme** temperatures, high **radiation**, and **microgravity**. Scientists explore how these things affect animals, plants, chemicals, and more. Sometimes, the astronauts themselves are the subjects of experiments!

US astronaut Peggy Whitson shows off soybeans grown on the International Space Station (ISS).

Scientists have grown vegetables, created oxygen, and even 3-D printed working tools, all while hundreds of miles high in the cosmos. These experiments and others teach scientists more about space every day!

OUT-OF-THIS-WORLD WORK WEEK

Astronaut scientists perform experiments aboard the International Space Station (ISS). In 2017, ISS astronauts set a record for time spent on science experiments. The team clocked ninety-nine hours of experiments in just one week!

Scott Kelly aboard the ISS

Astronaut's Body Stretches Out in Space

US astronaut Scott Kelly spent 340 days in space. He lived aboard the ISS from 2015 to 2016.

Kelly's year in space was one long experiment. Scientists wanted to see how space affected his body. Kelly has an **identical** twin brother. When Kelly returned to Earth, they compared several things about his body to his twin's.

Microgravity had stretched Kelly longer! He was now two inches (5 cm) taller than his twin. However, after Kelly adapted back to life on Earth, he shrank back to his former size.

Scott Kelly *(right)* and his twin, Mark

MICROGRAVITY TRANSFORMS ASTRONAUT'S GENES

When astronaut Scott Kelly returned home to Earth after his year in space, scientists compared his genes with his identical twin's. They found space travel had altered seven percent of Kelly's genes!

GETTING USED TO MICROGRAVITY

Adapting to microgravity can be tough. Astronauts can suffer from a lack of appetite, a stuffed-up nose, vomiting, and more while getting used to being in space.

NASA astronauts train in special microgravity aircraft and chambers.

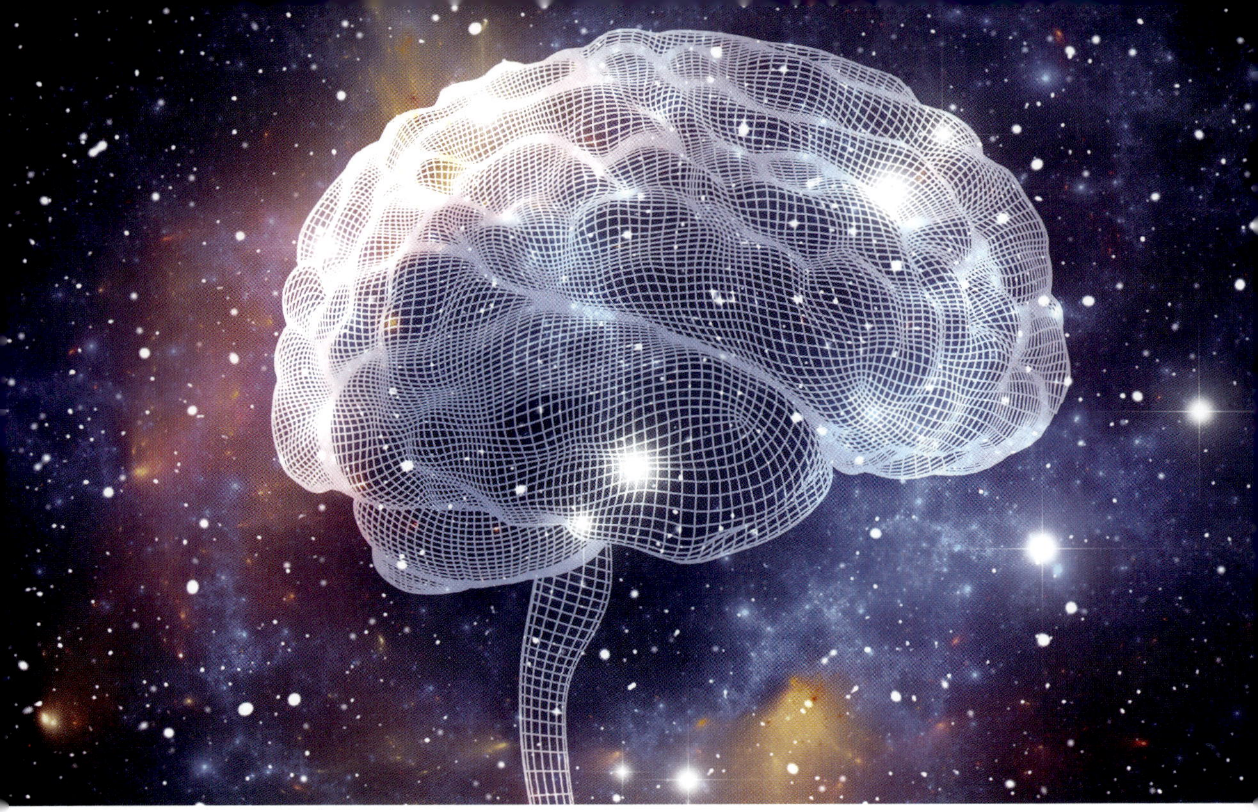

Space Squeezes Astronauts' Brains

In 2017, US scientist Rachael Seidler scanned the brains of thirty-four NASA astronauts. She found that the more time an astronaut had spent in space, the more likely it was that their brain changed.

These brain changes occurred because of shifting fluid. Microgravity causes fluid to move upward in the body. The brain becomes "squeezed" by the pressure this creates.

Seidler's team observed that over time, this space squeezing causes some astronauts' brains to **permanently** shift position within their skulls! What scientists have yet to discover is how dangerous these brain changes could be.

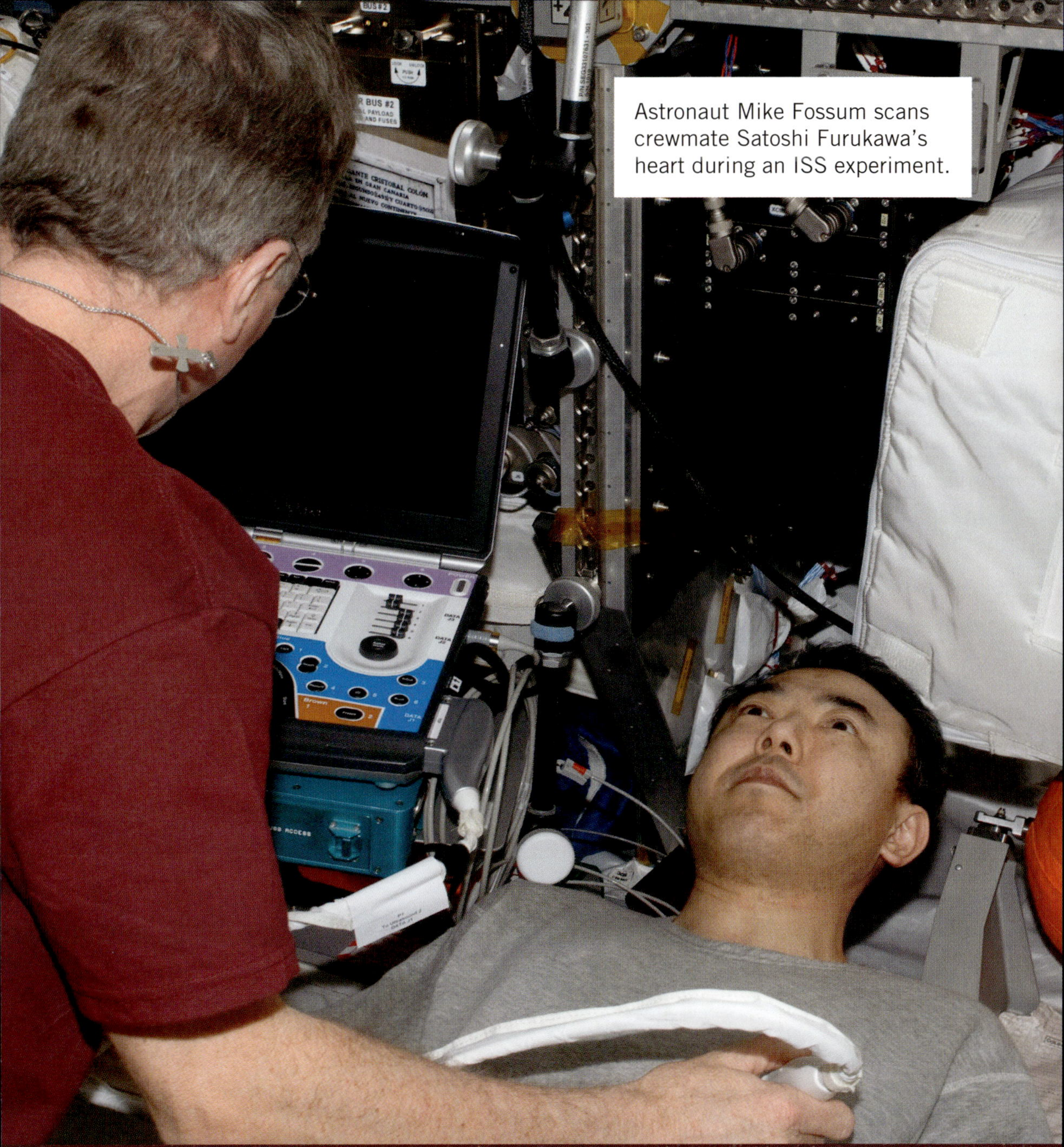

Astronaut Mike Fossum scans crewmate Satoshi Furukawa's heart during an ISS experiment.

A COSMIC CHANGE OF HEART

Scientists study how space affects the human heart. The heart doesn't have to work as hard to pump blood around the body in microgravity. This causes the organ to lose muscle mass. It also changes shape, becoming about nine percent rounder! Astronauts' hearts return to normal back on Earth.

A digital representation of a proposed Martian outpost

Mars Astronauts at Increased Cancer Risk

Radiation levels in space are much higher than on Earth. Radiation can cause **cancer**. So, astronauts are at a great risk the longer they are exposed.

Astronauts headed for Mars in the future will be especially at risk. It takes at least nine months to travel to the planet. This means nine months of increased radiation exposure. If any Mars astronauts develop cancer, scientists want to make sure treatments will work in microgravity.

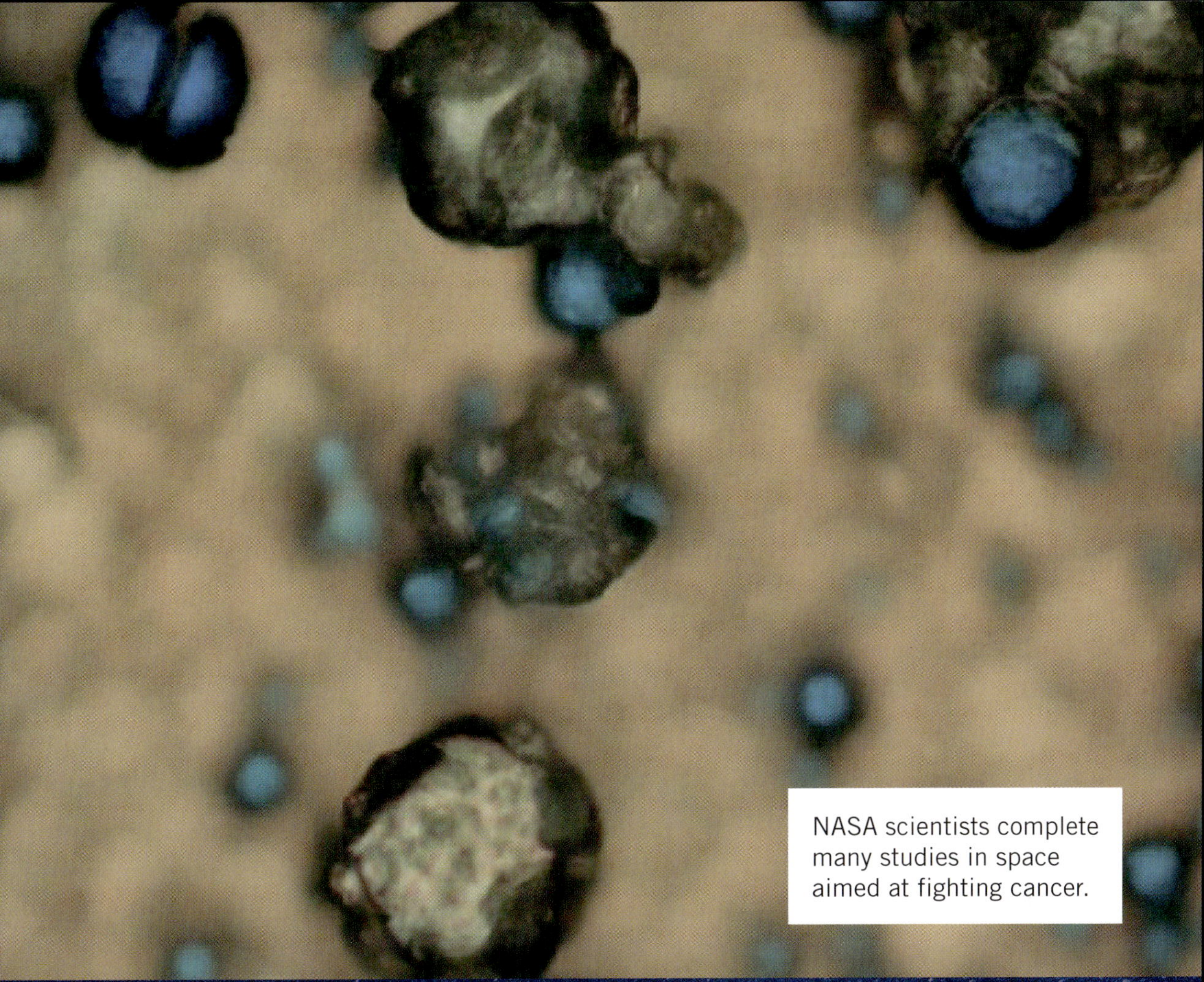
NASA scientists complete many studies in space aimed at fighting cancer.

ISS SCIENTISTS BATTLE CANCER IN THE COSMOS

Scientists on Earth have spent years studying cancer. This has included growing cancerous **tumors** in labs for study. Since 2003, scientists have grown these tumors in space too!

Space tumors are more like real tumors than those grown in labs on Earth. Without gravity, the space tumors grow large and **spherical**, the way they do inside the human body. One scientist compared a space tumor's shape to a tater tot, and an Earth tumor's to a pancake!

Scientists tested treatment drugs on the space tumors. Because the tumors' shapes were similar to those in the human body, the test results were more **accurate**.

Astronaut Scientist Becomes Space Farmer

In 2012, astronaut Don Pettit became a farmer in space. Pettit grew a zucchini plant aboard the ISS. He used **aeroponics** to grow the plant with very little soil or water.

The zucchini plant grew steadily, and also grew famous! Pettit tracked the plant's progress through NASA blog posts written from the zucchini's point of view. The plant became famous among Earth dwellers.

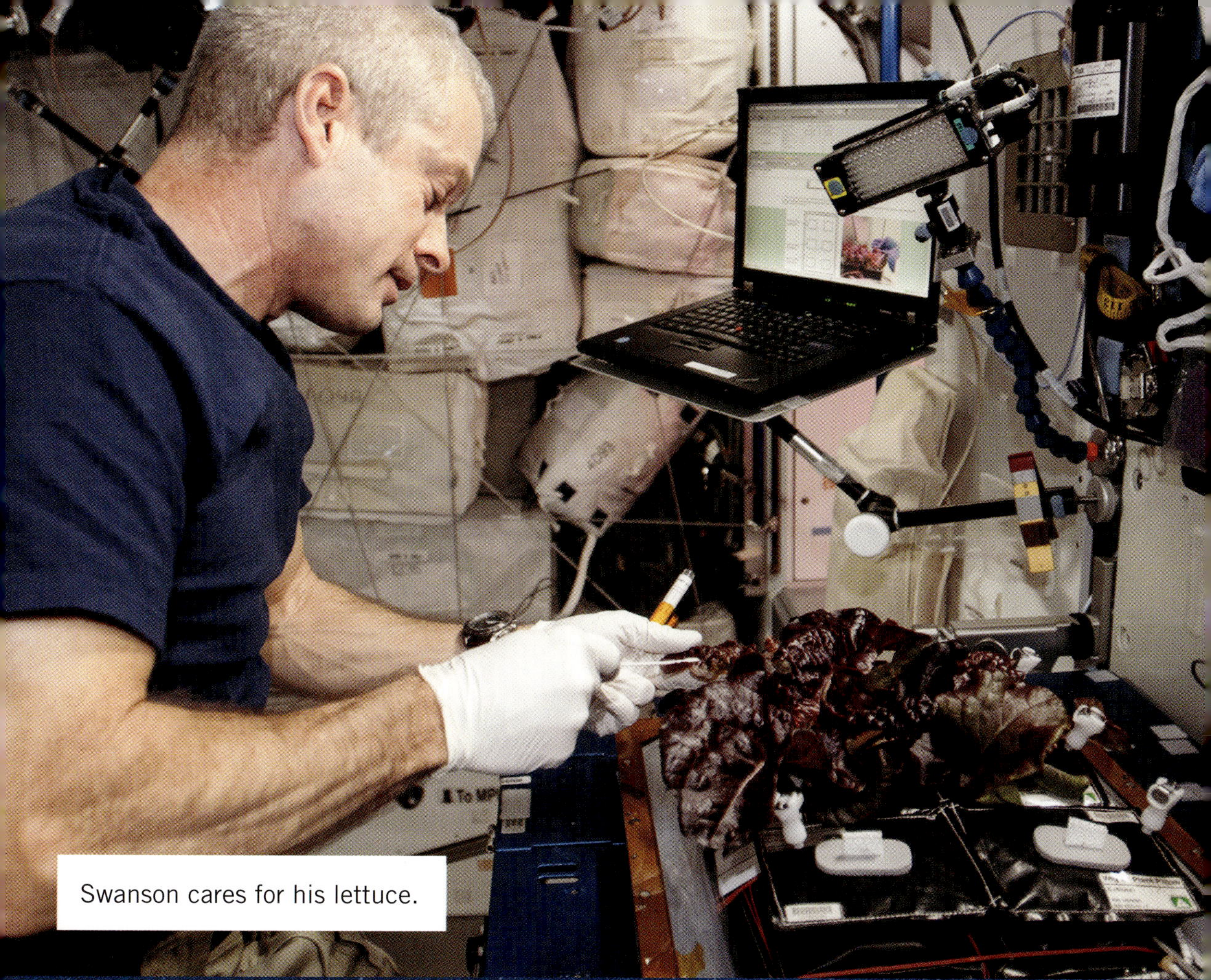

Swanson cares for his lettuce.

EATING LETTUCE GROWN IN ORBIT

In 2015, space-farmed food was on the ISS menu for the first time. Flight engineer Steve Swanson grew lettuce plants from seed to harvest. Half of the lettuce was packed away for study on Earth. The other half was eaten by Swanson and the crew.

FLOWERS SMELL DIFFERENT IN SPACE

In 1998, US scientist Braja Mookherjee sent a miniature rose aboard the space shuttle Discovery. The rose bloomed in space. But the space rose had produced fewer oils because of microgravity. So, the rose smelled differently than one grown on Earth!

Scientists Allow Ants to Invade the ISS

In 2013, NASA scientists brought about one hundred animals aboard the ISS. The small stowaways were cosmic ant colonies!

Ants are known for working together to sense their environment and search for food. Planned, patterned movements and walks are part of this process. Scientists wanted to see how microgravity affected it.

The ants had much less control over their movements when floating in space. Scientists used data from the ants to **predict** other patterned processes, such as robots programmed for search and rescue space missions.

Astronaut Rick Mastracchio watches the ants aboard the ISS.

Astronaut Mike Hopkins films the ISS ants.

SPACE ANTS INSPIRE EARTHLINGS

ISS scientists made their space ant experiment available for people on Earth to watch in real time via streamed video. Students across the United States were encouraged to perform their own ant farm experiments on Earth and compare them to the NASA study.

SpaceX travel posters imagine the company's visions of future tourism and life on Mars.

Pizza on Mars

Only robots had visited Mars as of 2018. But **entrepreneur** and scientist Elon Musk is working to change that! Musk is the founder of space flight company SpaceX. His life ambition is to help humankind colonize the solar system. Musk hopes SpaceX will one day offer private space travel to citizens of Earth. He envisions a future Mars city with homes, factories, and even pizza parlors!

SPACEX SENDS A CAR INTO ORBIT!

In February 2018, SpaceX did a test flight of its Falcon Heavy rocket. The rocket launched a car into space! The red convertible is SpaceX founder Elon Musk's car. A mannequin named Starman sits in the driver's seat. Starman and the car are **orbiting** the sun. Some scientists expect the car to remain in space for millions of years before crashing into anything!

A photo of Musk's car and Starman in space, taken by cameras mounted to the car

EXTRATERRESTRIAL OPINION

"What I'm trying to do is to make a significant difference in space flight and help make space flight accessible to almost anyone."

— SpaceX founder, Elon Musk

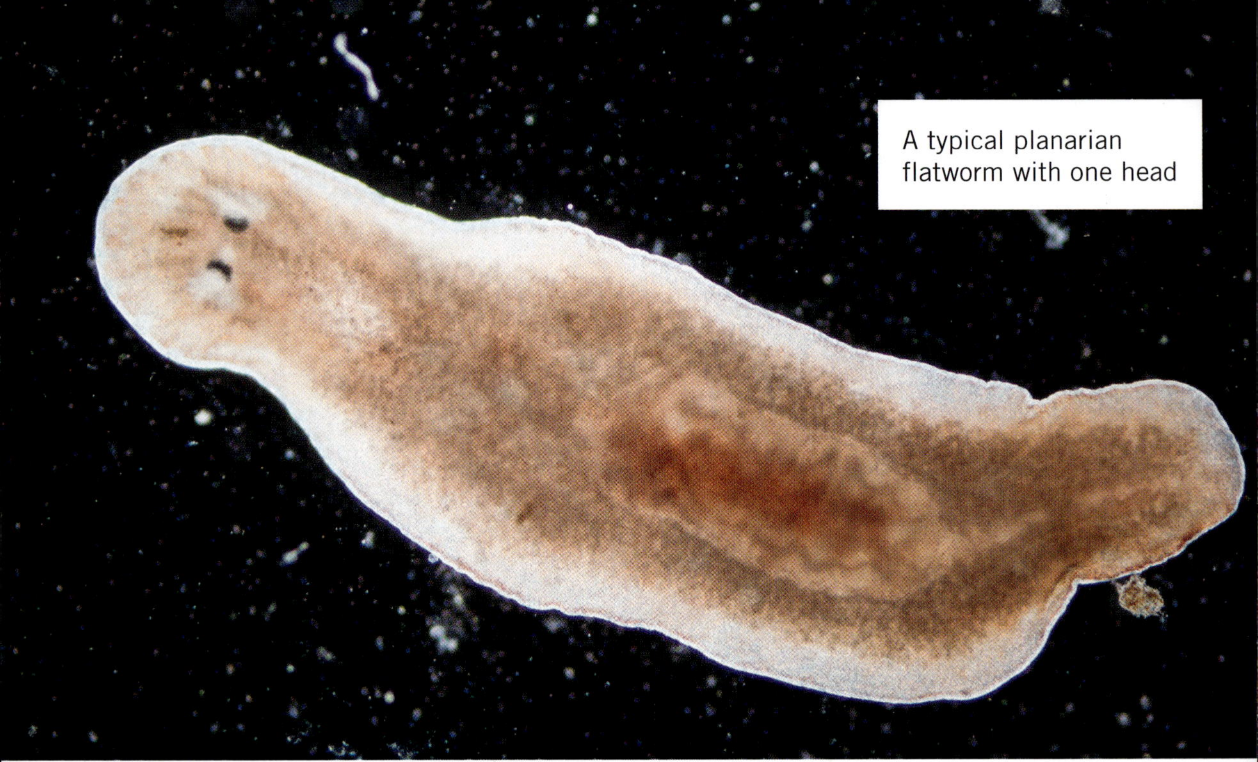

A typical planarian flatworm with one head

Cosmic Scientists Spawn Two-Headed Space Worms

Planarian flatworms are a type of worm of great interest to scientists. When this worm's head or tail is cut off, it grows back!

In 2014, Tufts University scientists cut the heads from several planarian flatworms and launched the bodies to space. ISS scientists watched the worm bodies grow new heads in microgravity. One worm grew back two heads instead of one! This was very rare. In eighteen years studying these worms on Earth, Tufts scientists had never seen it happen.

The space worm was sent back to Earth, where scientists chopped it in half again and again. Each time, the worm body grew two heads! Scientists think the absence of gravity and of Earth's magnetic fields caused this weird growing habit.

Baker with a model of the space shuttle Jupiter

Strelka (*right*) and Belka (*left*)

A cat models the type of equipment Félicette rode into space.

FURRY TAILS BLAZING TRAILS

Animals have a long history of helping scientists discover the mysteries of space. Several furry space pioneers beat 2014's wiggling worm colonies to the cosmos and returned safely to Earth.

Able and Baker: Monkeys that traveled safely to and from space in 1959

Strelka and Belka: Dogs that went into orbit and returned to Earth in 1960

Félicette: The first cat to visit space and return to Earth, in 1963

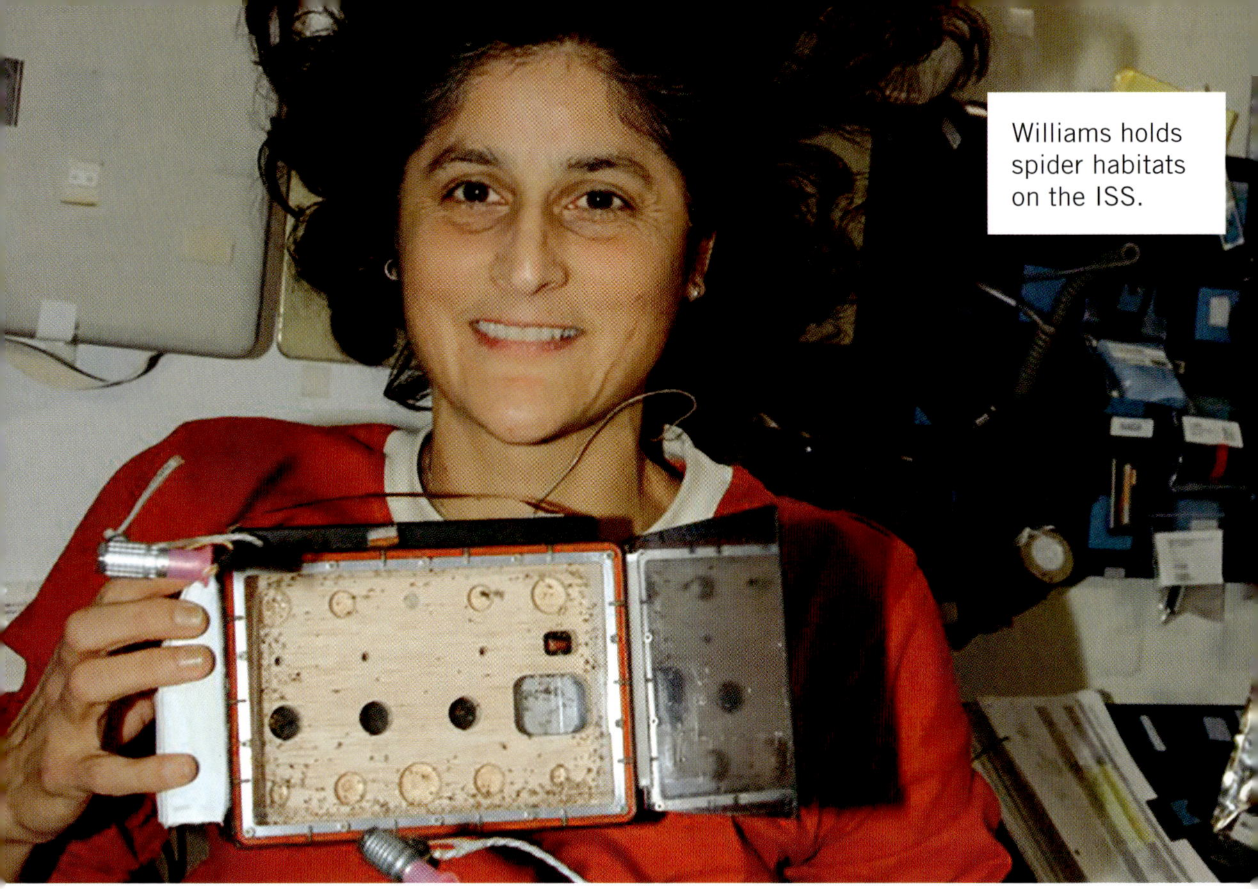

Williams holds spider habitats on the ISS.

Students Choose Scientists' Space Experiments

In 2011, space scientists launched a worldwide competition. Kids were asked to upload a two-minute video to YouTube describing a science experiment that could be done in space.

Organizers chose two videos out of the two thousand entries received! One was a video made by a student from Egypt. He created an experiment about jumping spiders. The other video was by two US students, who created an experiment about alien superbugs! Both experiments were carried out in space by NASA astronaut Sunita Williams. The results were livestreamed on YouTube for the world to watch.

The red-backed spider (*left*) and zebra spider (*right*) were two species NASA scientists brought to space.

STUDENT SPIDER EXPERIMENT SURPRISES SPACE SCIENTISTS

Amr Mohamed's experiment was one of two chosen by NASA to perform in space. Mohamed **hypothesized** that spider species that jump on their prey would not be able to hunt in microgravity. Scientists brought these spiders to the ISS, and Mohamed was proven wrong. Mohamed thought this was exciting! "I think it is boring when experiments turn out as expected," he said.

EXTRATERRESTRIAL OPINION

"The idea that something you made, something that's your experiment, being sent up into space and actually becoming a reality is pretty incredible."

—Dorothy Chen, US student whose alien superbug experiment was performed in space in 2012

Williams *(center, left)* with contest winners Amr Mohamed *(left)*, Dorothy Chen *(center, right)*, and Sara Ma

Galaxy's Coldest Science Lab Set Up on Space Station

Absolute zero is the coldest known temperature. It is so cold, scientists cannot create this temperature in a lab setting! However, a new space lab gets close.

The Cold Atom Laboratory (CAL) was launched to the ISS in May 2018. The lab is about the size of a refrigerator, but it gets much colder than one. CAL can reach a fraction of a degree above absolute zero.

Space scientists use CAL to study atom behavior at this extreme temperature. Atoms make up all things. And much of space is just slightly warmer than absolute zero. So, scientists can use CAL to learn a lot about how substances function in the freezing cold cosmos!

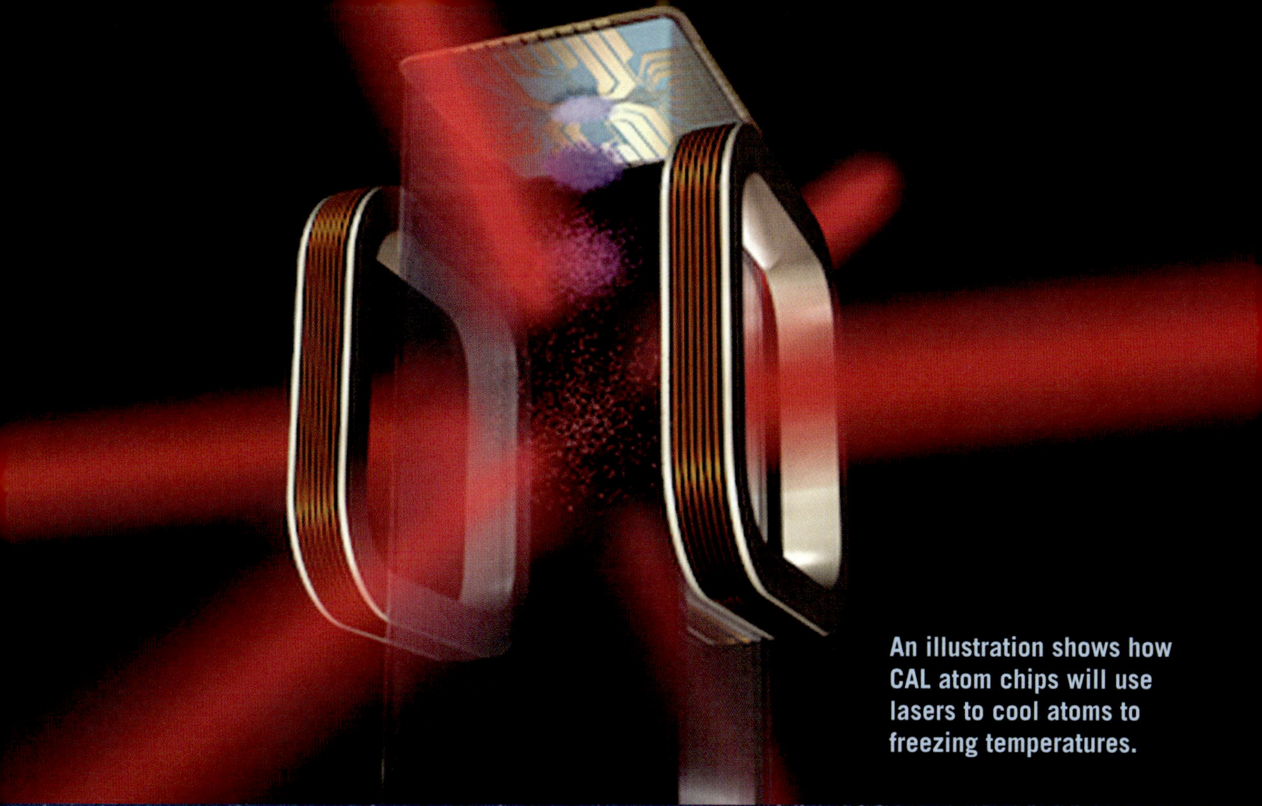

An illustration shows how CAL atom chips will use lasers to cool atoms to freezing temperatures.

SUPER COOL CAL TEAM

ISS scientists physically interact with CAL in space. But the lab also has a team of many scientists supporting it on Earth, from NASA's Jet Propulsion Laboratory.

Dr. David Aveline: CAL Team Leader, expert in planning and conducting physics experiments to develop space technology

Dr. Ethan Elliott: Developer of an Earth-bound CAL replica to help plan the space instrument's ISS mission

Dr. Jason Williams: Expert in measuring properties of atoms at low temperatures

From left to right: Aveline, Elliott, and Williams

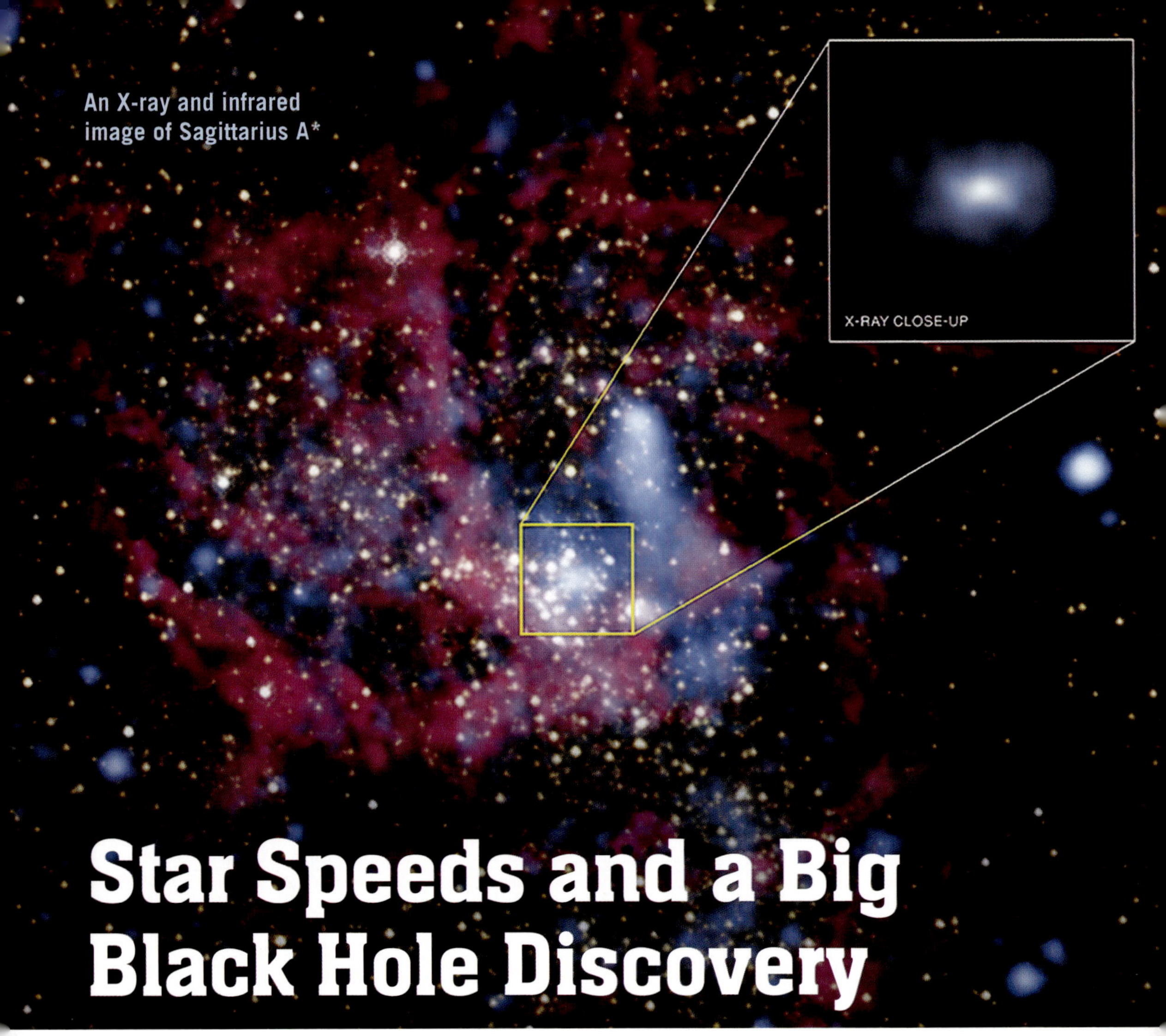

An X-ray and infrared image of Sagittarius A*

Star Speeds and a Big Black Hole Discovery

Our planet is in the Milky Way **galaxy**, which is vast. What's outside our galaxy? In 2003, UCLA scientist Andrea Ghez found out.

Ghez measured the speeds of stars moving close to the center of the galaxy and found they were moving very quickly. This suggested that they were orbiting something very large. This is because the larger an object is, the greater its gravitational pull on objects orbiting it.

Ghez decided the Milky Way rotates around a supermassive black hole! The black hole was named Sagittarius A*. This is pronounced "Sagittarius A-star."

SAGITTARIUS A* IS SUPER DENSE

Sagittarius A* is seventeen times larger in diameter than the sun. But the black hole has more than 4 million times the sun's mass!

An illustration of Sagittarius A*

EXTRATERRESTRIAL OPINION

"Stars have a life cycle. They're born. They live. And then the most massive stars end up as black holes. They [black holes] are defined by their immense, immense amounts of gravity. Gravity so intense that nothing can escape them, not even light."

—Andrea Ghez explaining black holes

Scientist Seager Hunts Habitable Planets

Sara Seager has made searching for another **habitable** planet her life's work. Seager is NASA's Deputy Science Director of TESS, launched in 2018.

TESS stands for Transiting Exoplanet Survey **Satellite**. The satellite used powerful cameras to search for faraway planets, especially those that are rocky and may have similar conditions to Earth.

An artist's illustration of TESS

EXTRATERRESTRIAL OPINION

". . . I envision that our descendants, hundreds of years from now, will embark on an interstellar journey to other worlds. And they will look back at all of us as the generation who first found the Earth-like worlds."

—Sara Seager, Deputy Science Director of TESS

Sara Seager

When planets pass in front of a star, they block the star's light. TESS will monitor the brightness of more than 200,000 stars, watching for shadows that could be caused by passing planets.

TESS is expected to find over 20,000 planets outside the solar system! Seager and her team will study them for Earth-like qualities that might allow alien life.

Cosmos Exclusive!

What's new and upcoming for scientists in space?

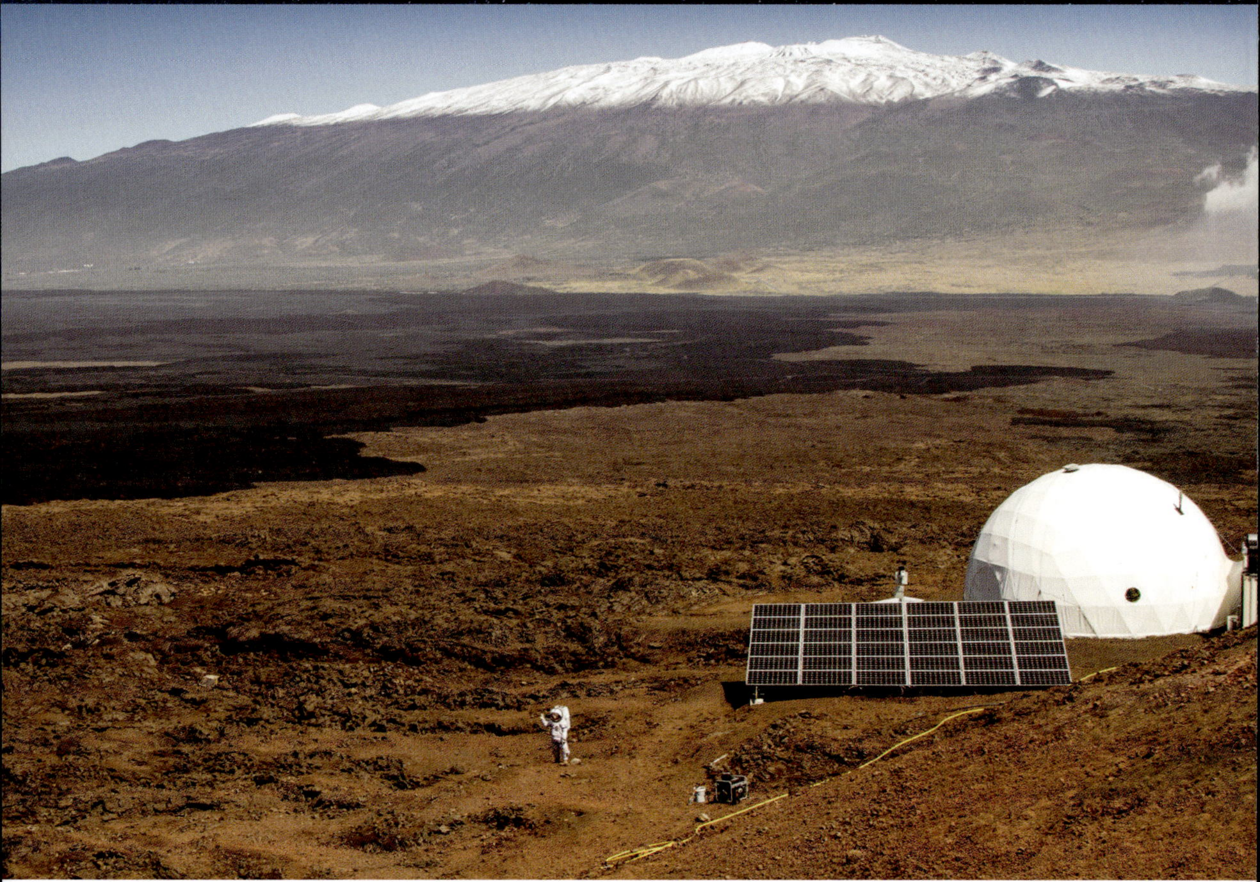

Simulating the Moon on Hawaiian Mountain

On the slopes of Mauna Loa, Hawaii, scientists simulated a moon colony habitat within a large plastic dome. Groups of people planned to live in the dome to experience many of the same living conditions moon colonists would. Scientists will study new technologies that might sustain life in space.

The Allen Telescope Array

Scientist Uses Massive Telescope to Seek Aliens

Astronomer Jill Tarter leads the Allen Telescope Array. The telescope searches the cosmos every day for signs of alien life. It is the only project of its kind to be completely devoted to searching for aliens.

EXTRATERRESTRIAL OPINION

"We should be looking for life beyond the earth because we want to understand what the laws of chemistry and physics have produced in this universe."

—Jill Tarter, Chair Emeritus for Search for Extraterrestrial Intelligence (SETI) research, SETI Institute

Glossary

accurate: correct in details

aeroponics: the process of growing plants in air without the use of soil

cancer: an often-deadly disease in which some cells in the body grow faster than normal cells and destroy healthy organs

entrepreneur: someone who organizes and starts businesses

extreme: existing in a high degree

galaxy: a very large group of stars and planets

habitable: safe and suitable for people to live in

hypothesized: suggested an idea that was to be tested using experiments

identical: exactly the same

microgravity: the near-absence of gravity in space

orbiting: traveling in a circular path around something, especially a planet or the sun

permanently: in a lasting way

predict: to say what will happen in the future

radiation: atomic particles that are sent out from a radioactive substance

satellite: a spacecraft that is sent into orbit around Earth or another body

spherical: having the form of a sphere, a solid form of a globe

tumors: abnormal lumps or masses of cells in the body

Further Information

BOOKS

Dickmann, Nancy. *Women Scientists in Astronomy and Space*. New York: Gareth Stevens, 2018.
Discover the space feats of many female scientists, astronauts, and astronomers throughout history.

Goldstein, Margaret J. *Astronauts: A Space Discovery Guide*. Minneapolis: Lerner Publications, 2017.
Learn more about the tasks astronauts complete in orbit, their daily schedule during missions, and how they stay healthy in space.

Owen, Ruth. *Astronaut: Life as a Scientist and Engineer in Space*. New York: Bearport, 2016.
Find out what it's like for scientists performing experiments and living aboard the International Space Station.

WEBSITES

The Kid Should See This—How Do Plants Grow in Space?
https://thekidshouldseethis.com/post/how-do-plants-grow-in-space-science-friday
Watch a video of astronauts growing plants in space to learn about the challenges and surprises of cosmic farming!

NASA Space Place—Mission Chronicles
https://spaceplace.nasa.gov/mission-chronicles/en/
Scientists who have traveled to space or worked on spacecraft answer questions about missions!

Science Kids—Astronaut Videos
http://www.sciencekids.co.nz/videos/astronauts.html
See astronauts living in space, where microgravity turns daily tasks into science experiments!

Index